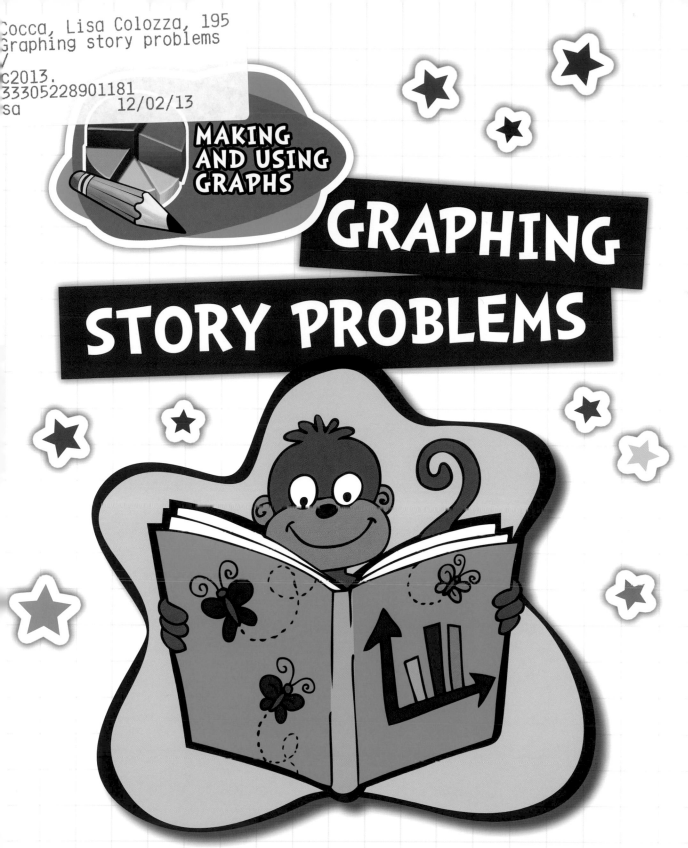

MAKING AND USING GRAPHS

GRAPHING STORY PROBLEMS

by Lisa Colozza Cocca   illustrated by Kathleen Petelinsek

CHERRY LAKE
Publishing

Published in the United States of America by Cherry Lake Publishing
Ann Arbor, Michigan
www.cherrylakepublishing.com

Consultants: Janice Bradley, PhD, Mathematically Connected Communities,
New Mexico State University; Marla Conn, Read-Ability

Editorial direction: Rebecca Rowell
Book design and illustration: The Design Lab

Photo credits: iStockphoto, 8, 16, 20; Ruslan Dashinsky/iStockphoto, 12

Library of Congress Cataloging-in-Publication Data
Cocca, Lisa Colozza, 1957–
  Graphing story problems / Lisa Colozza Cocca.
    p. cm. — (Making and using graphs)
  Audience: 005–007.
  Audience: Grades K to 3.
  Includes index.
  ISBN 978-1-61080-914-6 (hardback : alk. paper) — ISBN 978-1-61080-939-9
(paperback : alk. paper) — ISBN 978-1-61080-964-1 (ebook) —
ISBN 978-1-61080-989-4 (hosted ebook)
1. Word problems (Mathematics)—Graphic methods—Juvenile literature.
2. Mathematics—Graphic methods—Juvenile literature. I. Title.

  QA63.C55 2013
  511'.5—dc23

                              2012033603

Cherry Lake Publishing would like to acknowledge the work
of The Partnership for 21st Century Skills. Please visit
www.21stcenturyskills.org for more information.

Printed in the United States of America
Corporate Graphics Inc.
January 2013
CLFA10

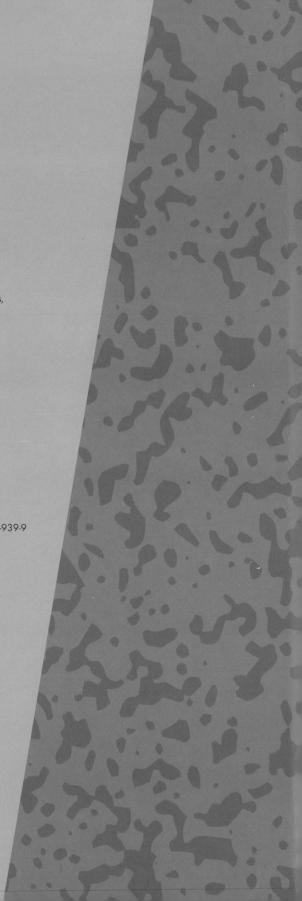

Table of Contents

CHAPTER ONE

What Are Graphs?

Graphs can tell stories about all kinds of things.

Do you like stories? **Graphs** are one way to tell stories. A graph is a kind of number picture. It can tell us how many we have of different things, such as balls, balloons, and backpacks. A graph can help us compare, too. It can answer questions about more, less, greater, fewer, most, and least.

Let's explore graphs and how they tell stories!

This is a bar graph:

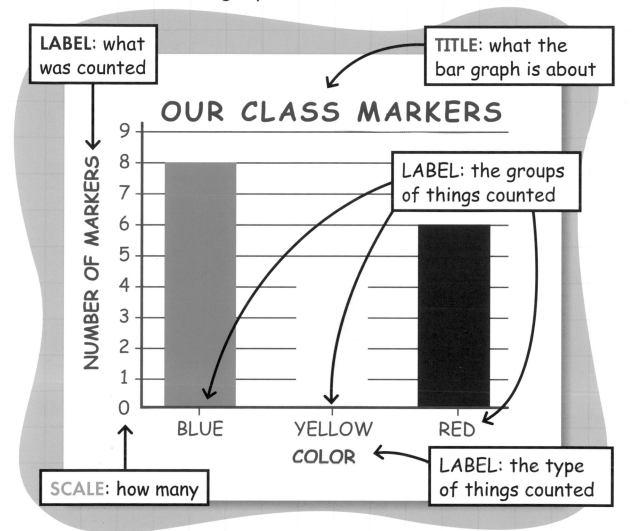

LABEL: what was counted

TITLE: what the bar graph is about

LABEL: the groups of things counted

SCALE: how many

LABEL: the type of things counted

OUR CLASS MARKERS

NUMBER OF MARKERS

9
8
7
6
5
4
3
2
1
0

BLUE   YELLOW   RED

COLOR

A bar is a rectangle. A bar graph uses bars to stand for the **data**. This graph is about our class markers. The label on the bottom is Colors. It shows the markers are sorted by color. How many blue markers are there?

We can show the same data in a pictograph. A pictograph is a bar graph that uses **symbols**, or pictures, instead of bars to show the data. A **key** tells us what the symbols stand for. Sometimes, the key is called a legend.

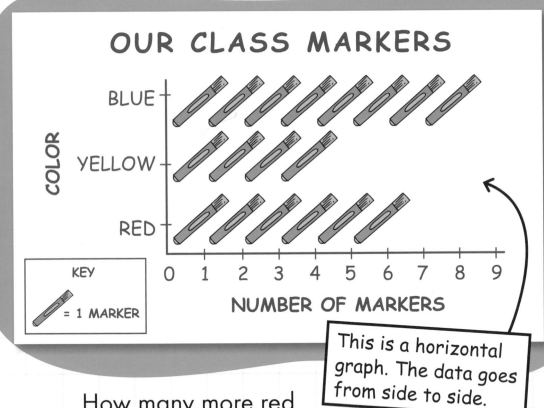

OUR CLASS MARKERS

This is a horizontal graph. The data goes from side to side.

How many more red markers than yellow markers are there?

We can also use graphs to show how things change over time. Let's see how many kids attended swim class each day for one week.

This is a line graph:

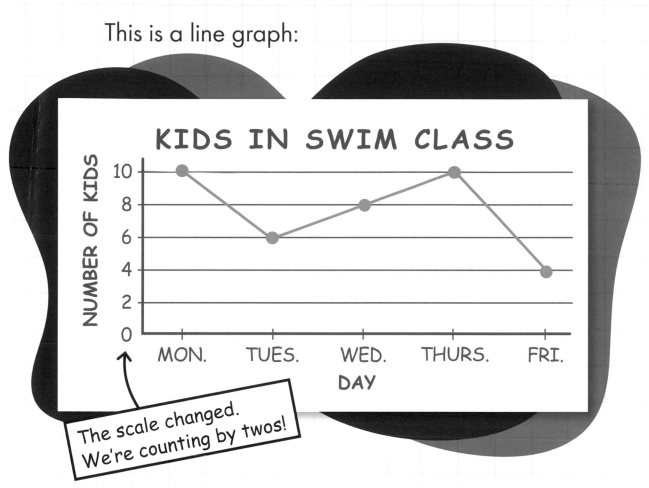

KIDS IN SWIM CLASS

The scale changed. We're counting by twos!

Each point on the line graph tells how many kids were in class on a certain day. The lines show if the number went up or down or stayed the same. The line between Thursday and Friday is going down. There were fewer students at swim class on Friday than on Thursday.

We can use graphs to help us solve story problems. Let's try some!

CHAPTER TWO

Graphing Beads

Let's graph bead colors!

Abby's best friend is having a birthday. Abby wants to make her a present. Her friend loves jewelry. Abby decides to make a necklace. She has a box of beads. She wants at least 12 beads of one color to make a bracelet. Abby sorts the beads by color.

It's time to pick colors. Let's help her!

First, we **record** our data in a **tally chart**. In a tally chart, we use tally marks to keep track of how many we've counted.

ABBY'S BEADS		
COLOR	NUMBER COUNTED	TOTAL
Red	|||||		6
White	||||| ||||| ||	12
Blue	||||| |||	8
Green	||||	4
Yellow	||||| ||	7
Pink	||||| |||	8
Purple	||||	4

The bead colors are listed at the left. Each color has its own **row**. We make a tally mark for each bead we count. The fifth mark goes across the other four.

After making tally marks, we count the marks in each row. We write the numbers in the chart.

Next, we use the data in our tally chart to make a bar graph.

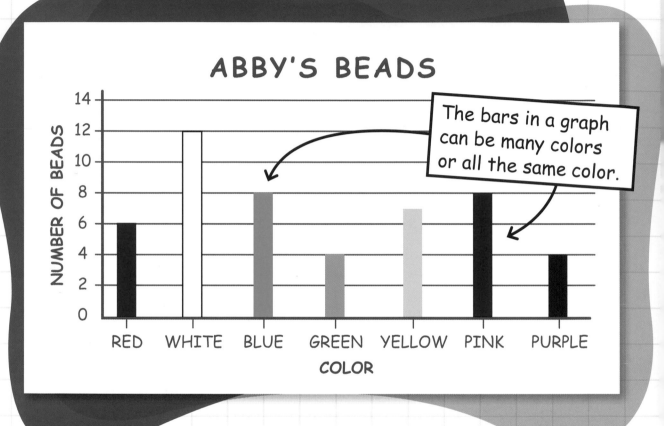

The bar graph shows how many of each color bead Abby has. Which color does she have 12 of?

Oh, no! Abby doesn't want a white necklace. Does she have enough beads to make a pink and purple necklace? How do you know?

ACTIVITY

Green and Yellow Beads

Abby wants to make a necklace for herself. Her favorite colors are green and yellow. Find out if she has enough beads in those colors to make a necklace. You may need paper and a pencil with an eraser to complete this activity.

INSTRUCTIONS:
1. Use the bar graph on page 10 to help you solve the problem. If you want, use the paper and pencil to note numbers and do the math.
2. How many yellow beads are there?
3. How many green beads are there?
4. How many green and yellow beads are there in all?
5. Abby needs 12 beads. Does she have enough?

To get a copy of this activity, visit www.cherrylakepublishing.com/activities.

CHAPTER THREE
Graphing Miles

Miles walked is one of the many things you can graph.

Do you belong to any clubs or groups? Daniel, Noah, and Mia belong to a walking group. They try to walk every day. They keep track of the number of miles they walk each week.

Daniel thinks he has walked the most miles this week. He wants to know for sure. Let's help him find out!

We'll begin by tallying the miles each person walked this week.

WALKING CLUB TOTALS FOR THE WEEK		
WALKER	MILES WALKED	TOTAL
Daniel	‖‖‖ ‖‖	9
Noah	‖‖	4
Mia	‖‖‖ ‖	

STOP!
Don't write in the book.

How many miles did Mia walk?

The left **column** has each person's name. The middle column has the tally marks. Each mark equals one mile. We need to add up the tally marks. We'll use the totals to create a graph.

Next, we make a pictograph with the data from our tally chart.

This pictograph is vertical. The data goes from bottom to top.

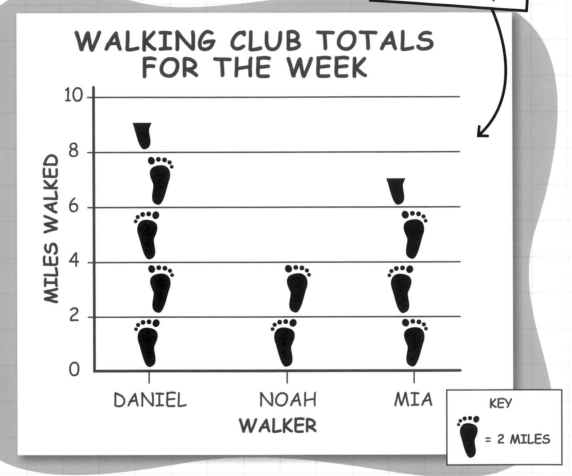

WALKING CLUB TOTALS FOR THE WEEK

MILES WALKED

DANIEL   NOAH   MIA
WALKER

KEY

= 2 MILES

The pictograph shows how many miles each person has walked. The key shows us one footprint stands for two miles. That means half of a footprint stands for one mile.

Is Daniel right? Did he walk the most miles?

14

ACTIVITY

Mia's Miles

Mia wants to know how many more miles she needs to walk to tie Daniel. You may need paper and a pencil with an eraser to complete this activity.

INSTRUCTIONS:
1. Use the pictograph on page 14 to help Mia find her answer.
2. How many miles did Daniel walk?
3. How many miles did Mia walk?
4. How many more miles does Mia need to walk to tie Daniel?

To get a copy of this activity, visit www.cherrylakepublishing.com/activities.

CHAPTER FOUR

Graphing Fish

We can count and graph fish by total number and by color.

Do you like animals? Visiting a pet store can be fun. Jacob visits one every day.

Jacob's family owns a pet shop. Jacob likes the fish most. He counts the fish every day before the store opens. The number keeps changing. People are buying the fish! Jacob wants to know how many fish the store sold on Tuesday.

The line graph shows how the number of fish changed during the week. Let's use it to help Jacob.

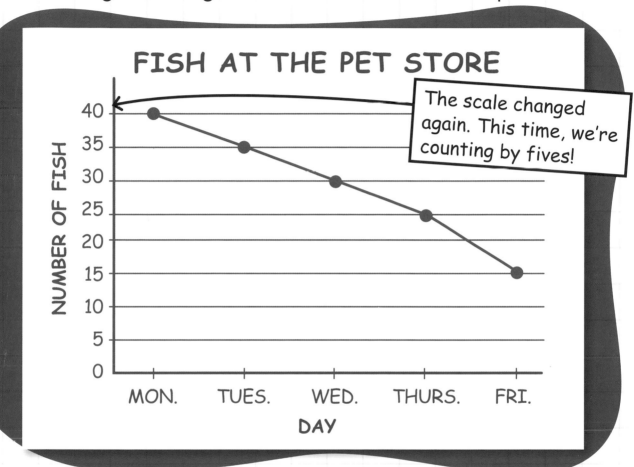

The line goes down between Tuesday and Wednesday. What does that tell us? Yes! Some fish were sold!

There were 35 fish in the tank on Tuesday morning. There were 30 fish on Wednesday morning. How many fish were sold on Tuesday?

Jacob decided to record the colors of fish in the tank on Thursday. He made a pie graph of his data. A pie graph is also known as a circle graph. It's a graph that shows data in a circle.

COLORS OF FISH
ON THURSDAY

■ ORANGE
■ BLACK
□ SILVER

The pie graph helps us easily see which color fish we have most of and least of.

What story does Jacob's pie graph tell? Which color of fish were there most of? Which were there least of?

Write a Story Problem

It's your turn to tell the story. You'll need paper and a pencil with an eraser to complete this activity.

INSTRUCTIONS:

1. Use the line graph on page 17 to write a story problem.
2. Remember, graphs tell us more, less, greater, fewer, most, and least. They tell us how many in one part or at a point of time and how many in all.
3. Write your problem on the paper.
4. Share your problem and the graph with a friend. Can your friend solve your problem using the graph?

To get a copy of this activity, visit www.cherrylakepublishing.com/activities.

CHAPTER FIVE

Graphs Are Fun

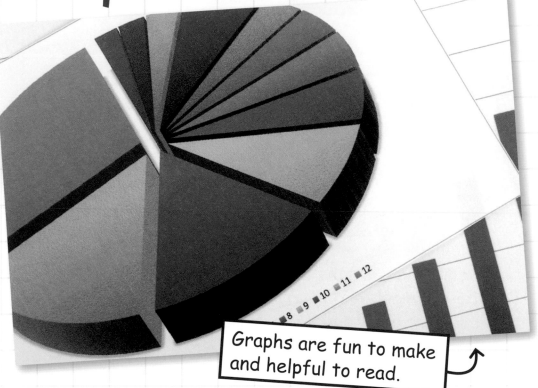

Graphs are fun to make and helpful to read.

There are many kinds of graphs. We've studied bar, line, and pie graphs. And don't forget tally charts and pictographs. Some graphs are great for comparing things. Others are better for showing how the number of something changed over time. What kind of graph do you like best?

Keep exploring graphs. You'll get better at reading them and making them. Try different colors, patterns, and symbols. Have fun!

Here are some other things you can do with graphs:

- Figure out which day in the summer was the hottest.
- Record which color vegetable you eat most often.
- Compare your friends' heights to determine which is tallest.
- Learn which kind of pet is most popular with the kids in your class.

We can tell all kinds of stories with graphs.

Glossary

column (KAH-luhm) a line of data that goes from top to bottom

data (DAY-tuh) information recorded about people or things

graph (graf) a diagram, or picture, that shows numbers

key (kee) a list or chart that tells what the pictures or symbols in a graph stand for; also called a legend

label (LAY-buhl) a name

record (ri-KORD) to write down

row (roh) a line of data that goes from side to side

scale (skale) a series of numbers that shows how many

symbol (SIM-buhl) a picture that stands for something else

tally chart (TAL-ee chahrt) a way to record things you count that uses tally marks

tally mark (TAL-ee mahrk) a line that stands for one item of something being counted

title (TYE-tuhl) the name of a chart

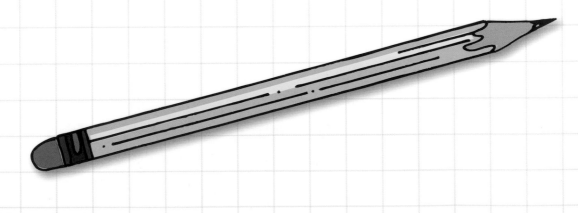

For More Information

BOOKS

Bodach, Vijaya Khisty. *Pictographs*. Mankato, MN: Capstone, 2008.

Leedy, Loreen. *The Great Graph Contest*. New York: Holiday House, 2005.

Piddock, Claire. *Line, Bar, and Circle Graphs*. New York: Crabtree, 2010.

WEB SITES

Beacon Learning Center—I Am Special!

www.beaconlearningcenter.com/WebLessons/IAmSpecial/me01.htm
Learn about what makes Rebecca special by reading pictographs about Rebecca and her friends.

Kids' Zone: Learning with NCES—Create a Graph Classic, Bar Graph

nces.ed.gov/nceskids/graphing/classic/bar.asp
Build a bar graph by filling in the labels and data. One click turns your data into a bar graph.

Math Is Fun—Data Graphs

www.mathsisfun.com/data/data-graph.php
Point and click to add and show data as a bar graph, line graph, pie graph, or data chart.

Index

About the Author

Lisa Colozza Cocca is a former teacher and school librarian. For the past decade, she has worked as a freelance writer and editor. She lives, works, and plays in New Jersey. Lisa thinks graphs are lots of fun.